M000201974

Except where otherwise indicated, all Scripture quotations are from the ESV® Bible (The Holy Bible, English Standard Version®), copyright © 2001 by Crossway, a publishing ministry of Good News Publishers. Used by permission. All rights reserved.

Scripture quotations marked NIV are taken from the Holy Bible, New International Version, Copyright © 1973, 1978, 1984 by the International Bible Society. Used by permission of Zondervan Bible Publishers.

THE BASIC GOSPEL

Copyright © 2018 Basic Gospel, Inc., Lewisville, TX 75057

ISBN 978-1-931899-44-4

All rights reserved. No portion of this book may be reproduced in any form without the written permission of Basic Gospel.

Printed in the United States of America.

THE BASIC GOSPEL

ESSENTIAL TRUTHS FOR YOU TO GROW IN GOD'S LOVE AND GRACE

BOB CHRISTOPHER

The Basic Gospel

Contents

The Basic Gospel

The basics.

Who wants to go back to the basics?

Shouldn't we go on to the deeper things of God?

Isn't that what the writer of Hebrews tells us to do?

"So let us **stop going over the basic teachings about Christ again and again. Let us go on instead and become mature in our understanding.** Surely we don't need to start again with the fundamental importance of repenting from evil deeds and placing our faith in God" Hebrews 6:1 (NLT).

So let's mature. Let's go deeper.

I agree, but let me ask you a question. Can you really mature if you don't have the basics right?

Can you go deeper into the love of God if you don't understand the cross, the place where God demonstrated His love for you?

Let me make a bold statement. **If you don't have the basics right, you will never grow and mature as a believer.**

On our daily radio broadcast we field questions about everything you can imagine. Our engineering team categorizes each call. The two issues people ask about the most are the forgiveness of sins and assurance of salvation.

Does this surprise you?

Doesn't every believer know that Christ died to forgive their sins? Doesn't every believer know they are eternally saved?

No they don't. And neither did I.

I received Christ when I was thirteen years of age. I responded to the good news that Christ died for my sins. But even though I knew this wonderful truth, doubt haunted me for many years. Fear and guilt joined the party as well.

I was deeply concerned about the forgiveness of my sins and the assurance of my salvation. Bottom line, I was confused about the basic Gospel message. I didn't know if I was forgiven or not; saved or not.

And I've met far too many Christians who are just as confused as I was. They know the words of the Gospel, but not the reality.

They call and ask questions like these.

Did Jesus die for all our sins, or just my past sins?

I understand that I've been forgiven for my sins... but if I deliberately sin do I need to ask God to forgive me?

Wouldn't God take away my pain if I was truly saved?

I'm constantly doubting God. Why isn't my life lining up with the Word of God?

I work all the time and I can't go to church. I feel like I'm a backslider and far away from God. Will I go to Hell because I am not out sharing the Gospel?

Where does this confusion come from and why is it so prevalent within Christian circles?

Unfortunately, often the confusion comes from the top. I know in my experience, I never heard any real, clear teaching on the meaning of Christ's death, burial and resurrection. I was hearing stuff, just not the right stuff.

This reminds me of the first year my daughter, Caitlin, played softball for a select team. She was so excited about playing. We hoped this would be a great experience for her. But it didn't turn out that way.

I remember one game in particular. The coach called on Caitlin to pinch hit. She had struggled at the plate the whole year. Every game seemed to be another step back for her.

She walked to the plate and stepped into the box. I was praying. Her mom was praying. And all the other parents were crossing their fingers in hopes she would get a hit. But it was not to be. She struck out again. She turned and marched back to the dugout with a face filled with disappointment and frustration. Everyone in the stands felt her pain.

After the game, several dads beelined to Caitlin to "help" her with her swing. Caitlin soaked in everything these dads said. She wanted to get better. And she was willing to try anything that might help. So she listened.

"Hold your hands higher."

"Turn your hips more."

"Stay on your backside."

"Keep your hands inside the ball."

All of this advice made Caitlin's head spin. This "good" instruction didn't help at all. It made matters worse. These well intentioned dads did nothing but confuse Caitlin and add to her frustration.

Let me tell you. I was really glad when we moved on from that nightmare. Once we did, we found a hitting coach that anchored Caitlin's swing to the basic fundamentals. From that point, her softball career exploded. She was a force to be reckoned with every time she stepped into the batter's box.

Based on what I've encountered through our daily radio program, there is not a lot of difference between Caitlin's experience her first year in the softball world and that of the vast majority of believers.

They struggle to get the Christian life right. They are filled with frustration and disappointment. They listen to anything that might help, that just might put all the pieces together. They listen to stuff, just not the right stuff.

They know how to "be more", "do more", and "have more." They know the side of the aisle to stand on politically and how to vote on key issues. They know lots of good information, but they don't know the basic Gospel.

One of our radio listeners put it this way, "I have heard the Gospel a gillion times, but it has always had some sort of strings attached that effectually muted its clarity." As Paul wrote in Galatians, "this is really no Gospel at all."

And if it's not the Gospel, it's not good news.

Our parched hearts and weary souls need good news. Nothing else will meet our deepest needs, or anchor us to the foundation of God's love and grace.

But that's not what the vast majority of believers get. Instead of awing us with Christ's magnificent achievement on our behalf, most teachers and preachers spend the bulk of their time telling us what we need to do for God.

But what if we don't do all the stuff they tell us it takes to be good Christians?

What if we don't tithe?

What if we don't go to church every Sunday?

What if we fail to share Jesus with that guy we rode the elevator with?

What if we don't confess every sin we commit?

What if we don't read our Bible every day?

What if we still have crazy thoughts and evil desires?

What if we actually choose to give in to temptation?

All these "rah rah, go do good things for Jesus messages" may sound good. But boy do they raise a lot of "what ifs," which do to us exactly what those dads did to Caitlin –

keep our minds swirling with confusion and blind us to the simple, powerful, life-changing message of Jesus Christ.

Such was the case for Mark. Driving to work one day, he happened upon our radio broadcast. He was intrigued by the conversations with the callers. But what really caught his ear was the simple, basic explanation of the Gospel. He wrote this encouraging note after listening for a while.

"I felt like I was being unshackled from a lifetime of trying and never feeling like I was adequate enough to 'please' God. I just didn't understand how anyone could possibly live up to what I thought were the expectations of being a good Christian.

I realize now that our salvation hinges not on 'works' but on the gospel – the death, burial and resurrection of Jesus, and that He died for our sins ... once and for all. How many times I must have read this in the Bible before; and for some reason I just never grasped these truths and realities."

Maybe you are where Mark was. You are confused and struggling to fit all the pieces together. Let me tell you. There is hope and there are answers. You don't have to live confused or fearful or frustrated. The basic Gospel can clear away your confusion and unshackle you from a lifetime of trying to "please" God.

But what is the basic Gospel? Here, let me share two key passages to set the stage.

The first is 1 Corinthians 3:11 (NIV): "For no one can lay any foundation other than the one already laid, which is **Jesus Christ**." When we talk about the Gospel, we are really talking about Jesus. He is God's good news to us. This is the truth we learn in the Christmas story. The message given to the shepherds was this; "Do not be afraid. I bring you good news of great joy that will be for all the people. Today in the town of David a savior has been born to you. He is Christ the Lord" Luke 2:10, 11(NIV). What we need in life is the good news about Jesus. What I've learned is that this is a story we never tire of hearing. It is the story that brings great joy to our hearts.

The second passage is 1 Corinthians 15:1-4 (NIV): "Now, brothers, I want to remind you of the gospel I preached to you, which you received and on which you have taken your stand. By this gospel you are saved, if you hold firmly to the word I preached to you. Otherwise, you have believed in vain. For what I received I passed on to you as of first importance: that Christ died for our sins according to the Scriptures, that He was buried, that He was raised on the third day according to Scriptures..."

Here again the Gospel is Jesus—His death, His burial, His resurrection. Notice that Paul describes the Gospel as that which is of first importance. NT Wright, a wonderful theologian and writer had this to say about the Apostle Paul, "The gospel, the gospel, the gospel. It defined Paul. It defined his work."

For Paul, the Gospel was primary. It was that one big thing. And it can be for you, as well. This good news story of Jesus can be your story.

An Invitation

This book is an invitation to you to take a fresh look at the basic Gospel message.

This invitation is not without precedence. Getting back to the basics has spawned many of the revivals and spiritual awakenings history has recorded especially in the United States. In the Great Awakening that took place in the 1700's, George Whitfield led the charge with his renewed focus on salvation by grace through faith. In the sixties and seventies, a wave of evangelism swept over the country as leaders once again focused on the simple, powerful message of the Gospel.

Even today, the basics of Christianity are trending favorably. Back in the 90's, a publishing executive said a book with "grace" in the title would never sell. Now, "grace" dons the covers of many of the best-selling Christian books. And much of what I see and read online is about the simple Gospel message as well. I think this is the case today because life on every front is messy, chaotic and confusing.

Whenever life gets messy, chaotic, or confusing, the wise get back to the basics. This is true in every arena of life. To right the ship, you have to get back to the fundamentals.

Vince Lombardi did just that when he took over the helm for the Green Bay Packers. This team struggled through ten straight losing seasons. The fan base was sick and tired of being thought of as "loserville." Something had to change.

Lombardi ran his first few practices just as he had done for his previous teams. After a few days, his enthusiasm turned to frustration as he watched his players practice. They couldn't do anything right.

One particular day, Lombardi had had enough. He blew his whistle. "Everybody stop and gather around," he yelled. Then he knelt down, picked up the pigskin, and said, "Let's start at the beginning. This is a football. These are the yard markers. I'm the coach. You are the players." He went back to the basics.

Under Lombardi's leadership, the players quickly learned that even at the highest level of competition, mastering the basics of the game and executing them on the field is the key to success. Within a short period of time, the Green Bay Packers were on top of the football world, winning the first two super bowls ever played.

Lombardi is legendary. Some call him the greatest coach to ever live. Why? Because he was a man dedicated to teaching the basics of football and motivating his team to carry them out in every game.

Maybe its time that we take a fresh look at the basics.

So gather around. Let's start at the beginning. This is...

The Basic Gospel

This Is Jesus...

Jesus is God

In the beginning was the Word, and the Word was with God, and the Word was God.

John 1:1 (NIV)

Jesus said to them, "Truly, truly, I say to you, before Abraham was, I am."

John 8:58

He is the radiance of the glory of God and the exact imprint of his nature, and he upholds the universe by the word of his power. After making purification for sins, he sat down at the right hand of the Majesty on high

Hebrews 1:3

God's Name

You remember the story of Moses and the burning bush. Exodus 3 is where you find it. Well God is the fire in the bush. He called out to Moses and said...

"Come, I will send you to Pharaoh that you may bring my people, the children of Israel, out of Egypt. "

Moses asked God, what if "they ask me, 'What is his name?' what shall I say to them?"

God said to Moses, "I AM who I AM. Say this to the people, I am has sent me to you."

I AM. That's God's name. And that's Jesus's name. Why? Because Jesus is God.

Jesus is Fully Man

And the Word became flesh and dwelt among us, and we have seen his glory, glory as of the only Son from the Father, full of grace and truth.

John 1:14

Have this mind among yourselves, which is yours in Christ Jesus, who, though he was in the form of God, did not count equality with God a thing to be grasped, but emptied himself, by taking the form of a servant, being born in the likeness of men. And being found in human form, he humbled himself by becoming obedient to the point of death, even death on a cross.

Philippians 2:5-8

Jesus is both fully God and fully man.

For in him the whole fullness of deity dwells bodily.
Colossians 2:9

Jesus is Savior

For unto you is born this day in the city of David a Savior, who is Christ the Lord.

Luke 2:11

Our great God and Savior Jesus Christ.

Titus 2:13b

Jesus is High Priest

This becomes even more evident when another priest arises in the likeness of Melchizedek, who has become a priest, not on the basis of a legal requirement concerning bodily descent, but by the power of an indestructible life. For it is witnessed of him, "You are a priest forever, after the order of Melchizedek."

Hebrews 7:15-17

For we do not have a high priest who is unable to sympathize with our weaknesses, but one who in every respect has been tempted as we are, yet without sin. Let us then with confidence draw near to the throne of grace, that we may receive mercy and find grace to help in time of need.

Hebrews 4:15, 16

The former priests were many in number, because they were prevented by death from continuing in office, but he holds his priesthood permanently, because he continues forever. Consequently, he is able to save to the uttermost those who draw near to God through him, since he always lives to make intercession for them.

Hebrews 7:23-25

Jesus is the Resurrection and the Life

Jesus said to her, "I am the resurrection and the life. Whoever believes in me, though he die, yet shall he live, and everyone who lives and believes in me shall never die. Do you believe this?"

John 11:25, 26

And this is the testimony, that God gave us eternal life, and this life is in his Son. Whoever has the Son has life; whoever does not have the Son of God does not have life.

1 John 5:11, 12

Jesus is Lord

Concerning his Son, who was descended from David according to the flesh and was declared to be the Son of God in power according to the Spirit of holiness by his resurrection from the dead, Jesus Christ our Lord.

Romans 1:3, 4

If you confess with your mouth that Jesus is Lord and believe in your heart that God raised him from the dead, you will be saved.

Romans 10:9

The Invitation

But these are written so that you may believe that Jesus is the Christ, the Son of God, and that by believing you may have life in his name.

John 20:31

But to all who did receive him, who believed in his name, he gave the right to become children of God, who were born, not of blood nor of the will of the flesh nor of the will of man, but of God.

John 1:12, 13

Come to me, all who labor and are heavy laden, and I will give you rest. Take my yoke upon you, and learn from me, for I am gentle and lowly in heart, and you will find rest for your souls. For my yoke is easy, and my burden is light."

Matthew 11:28-30

The Basic Gospel

This Is Grace...

Grace is Powerful, Personal, Intelligent, and Active

For the grace of God that brings salvation has appeared to all men. It teaches us to say "No" to ungodliness and worldly passions, and to live self-controlled, upright and godly lives in this present age, while we wait for the blessed hope—the glorious appearing of our great God and Savior, Jesus Christ, who gave himself for us to redeem us from all wickedness and to purify for himself a people that are his very own, eager to do what is good.

Titus 2:11-14 (NIV)

**Grace is Found in the Person
and Work of Jesus Christ**

From the fullness of his grace we have all received one
blessing after another. For the law was given through
Moses; grace and truth came through Jesus Christ.
John 1:16, 17 (NIV)

To know the wonders of grace
look to Jesus.

Grace Makes us Alive in Christ

But because of his great love for us, God, who is rich in
mercy, made us alive with Christ even when we were dead
in transgressions—it is by grace you have been saved.
And God raised us up with Christ and seated us with him
in the heavenly realms in Christ Jesus, in order that in the
coming ages he might show the incomparable riches of
his grace, expressed in his kindness to us in Christ Jesus.
For it is by grace you have been saved, through faith—
and this not from yourselves, it is the gift of God—not by
works, so that no one can boast.

Ephesians 2:4-9 (NIV)

Grace Justifies, Redeems and Forgives

There is no difference, for all have sinned and fall short of the glory of God, and are justified freely by his grace through the redemption that came by Christ Jesus.

Romans 3:22-24 (NIV)

In him we have redemption through his blood, the forgiveness of our trespasses, according to the riches of his grace ...

Ephesians 1:7 (NIV)

The Christian life is by grace through faith in Jesus from start to finish.

Grace Reigns

The law was added so that the trespass might increase. But where sin increased, grace increased all the more, so that, just as sin reigned in death, so also grace might reign through righteousness to bring eternal life through Jesus Christ our Lord.

Romans 5:20, 21 (NIV)

Grace Freed Us from Sin's Power

For sin shall not be your master, because you are not under law, but under grace.

Romans 6:14 (NIV)

Grace is Sufficient in All Circumstances

But he said to me, "My grace is sufficient for you, for my power is made perfect in weakness." Therefore I will boast all the more gladly about my weaknesses, so that Christ's power may rest on me.

2 Corinthians 12:9 (NIV)

Grace is the Power for Life

But by the grace of God I am what I am, and his grace toward me was not in vain. On the contrary, I worked harder than any of them, though it was not I, but the grace of God that is with me.

1 Corinthians 15:10 (NIV)

Grow in Grace

But grow in the grace and knowledge of our Lord and Savior Jesus Christ. To him be glory both now and forever! Amen.

2 Peter 3:18 (NIV)

The grace of the Lord Jesus be with all. Amen.

Revelation 22:21 (NIV)

This Is the
New Covenant...

The New is Superior to The Old

For if there had been nothing wrong with that first covenant, no place would have been sought for another. But God found fault with the people...

Hebrews 8:7, 8 (NIV)

For when there is a change of the priesthood, there must also be a change of the law.

Hebrews 7:12 (NIV)

The former regulation is set aside because it was weak and useless (for the law made nothing perfect), and a better hope is introduced, by which we draw near to God.

Hebrews 7:18, 19 (NIV)

The New Covenant

The New Covenant was prophesied
by Jeremiah when he wrote,
"The time is coming…"

When Jesus raised the cup at the Last Supper
he boldly proclaimed,
"The time is now!"

The New was Ratified by Jesus

In the same way, after the supper he [Jesus] took the cup,
saying, "This cup is the new covenant in my blood, which
is poured out for you."

Luke 22:20 (NIV)

For this reason Christ is the mediator of a new covenant,
that those who are called may receive the promised
eternal inheritance—now that he has died as a ransom
to set them free from the sins committed under the first

covenant. In the case of a will, it is necessary to prove the death of the one who made it, because a will is in force only when somebody has died; it never takes effect while the one who made it is living.

Hebrews 9:15–17 (NIV)

Then he said, "Here I am, I have come to do your will." He sets aside the first to establish the second. And by that will, we have been made holy through the sacrifice of the body of Jesus Christ once for all. Day after day every priest stands and performs his religious duties; again and again he offers the same sacrifices, which can never take away sins. But when this priest had offered for all time one sacrifice for sins, he sat down at the right hand of God.

Hebrews 10:9-12 (NIV)

> *At the cross Jesus fulfilled the old covenant and ushered in the new covenant.*

The New is for Everyone

What if he did this to make the riches of his glory known to the objects of his mercy, whom he prepared in advance for glory— even us, whom he also called, not only from the Jews but also from the Gentiles? As he says in Hosea: "I will call them 'my people' who are not my people; and I will call her 'my loved one' who is not my loved one,"

Romans 9:23–25 (NIV)

For he himself is our peace, who has made the two one and has destroyed the barrier, the dividing wall of hostility, by abolishing in his flesh the law with its commandments and regulations. His purpose was to create in himself one new man out of the two, thus making peace...

Ephesians 2:14, 15 (NIV)

The New Contains Four Eternal Promises

1. *"I will put my laws in their minds and write them on their hearts."* Hebrews 8:10a (NIV)

   Obedience is now the inside-out result of grace: the indwelling Holy Spirit.

2. *"I will be their God, and they will be my people."* Hebrews 8:10b (NIV)

   We are in permanent relationship with God through Jesus.

3. *"...because they will all know me, from the least of them to the greatest..."* Hebrews 10:11 (NIV) *"Now this is eternal life: That they may know you, the only true God, and Jesus Christ, whom you have sent."* John 17:3 (NIV)

   We have eternal life.

4. *"For I will forgive their wickedness and will remember their sins no more."* Hebrews 8:12 (NIV)

   Sin has been defeated once and for all.

The New is Guaranteed by Jesus

Because God wanted to make the unchanging nature of his purpose very clear to the heirs of what was promised, he confirmed it with an oath. God did this so that, by two unchangeable things in which it is impossible for God to lie, we who have fled to take hold of the hope offered to us may be greatly encouraged. We have this hope as an anchor for the soul, firm and secure.

Hebrews 6:17–19 (NIV)

Because of this oath, Jesus has become the guarantee of a better covenant.

Hebrews 7:22 (NIV)

The New is a Ministry of Life and Freedom

He has made us competent as ministers of a new covenant—not of the letter but of the Spirit; for the letter kills, but the Spirit gives life.

2 Corinthians 3:6 (NIV)

Now the Lord is the Spirit, and where the Spirit of the Lord is, there is freedom. And we, who with unveiled faces all reflect the Lord's glory, are being transformed into his likeness with ever-increasing glory, which comes from the Lord, who is the Spirit.

2 Corinthians 3:17, 18 (NIV)

The New Promises Rest

Therefore, since the promise of entering his rest still stands, let us be careful that none of you be found to have fallen short of it. For we also have had the gospel preached to us, just as they did; but the message they heard was of no value to them, because those who heard did not combine it with faith. Now we who have believed enter that rest...

Hebrews 4:1–3 (NIV)

There remains, then, a Sabbath-rest for the people of God; for anyone who enters God's rest also rests from his own work, just as God did from his. Let us, therefore, make every effort to enter that rest, so that no one will fall by following their example of disobedience.

Hebrews 4:9–11 (NIV)

You are a new covenant believer!
Because of the cross
you live in the New, not the Old.

This is Forgiveness...

Jesus Forgives Sin

Who can forgive sins but God alone? Immediately Jesus knew in his spirit that this was what they were thinking in their hearts, and he said to them, "Why are you thinking these things? Which is easier: to say to this paralyzed man, 'Your sins are forgiven,' or to say, 'Get up, take your mat and walk'? But I want you to know that the Son of Man has authority on earth to forgive sins. So he said to the man, "I tell you, get up, take your mat and go home."

Mark 2:7-11 (NIV)

Forgiveness Requires the Shedding of Blood

Indeed, under the law almost everything is purified with blood, and without the shedding of blood there is no forgiveness of sins.

Hebrews 9:22

Jesus Shed His Blood Once For All Time

For Christ has entered, not into holy places made with hands, which are copies of the true things, but into heaven itself, now to appear in the presence of God on our behalf. Nor was it to offer himself repeatedly, as the high priest enters the holy places every year with blood not his own, for then he would have had to suffer repeatedly since the foundation of the world. But as it is, he has appeared once for all at the end of the ages to put away sin by the sacrifice of himself.

Hebrews 9:24-26

And every priest stands daily at his service, offering repeatedly the same sacrifices, which can never take away sins. But when Christ had offered for all time a single sacrifice for sins, he sat down at the right hand of God.

Hebrews 10:11, 12

For Christ also suffered once for sins, the righteous for the unrighteous, that he might bring us to God.

1 Peter 3:18

Jesus Forgave All Your Sins

When you were dead in your sins and in the uncircumcision of your flesh, God made you alive with Christ. He forgave us all our sins, having canceled the charge of our legal indebtedness, which stood against us and condemned us; he has taken it away, nailing it to the cross.

Colossians 2:13, 14 (NIV)

Forgiveness

It means…

– To send away
– To dismiss, or put away
– To remove
– To let go from one's further notice or care

Jesus removed your sins.
He sent them away once and for all.
And now he remembers your sins no more.

Then he adds: "Their sins and lawless acts I will remember no more." And where these have been forgiven, sacrifice for sin is no longer necessary.

Hebrews 10:17, 18 (NIV)

I am writing to you, dear children, because your sins have been forgiven on account of his name.

1 John 2:12 NIV)

Forgiveness is in Christ

All the prophets testify about him that everyone who believes in him receives forgiveness of sins through his name.

Acts 10:43 (NIV)

For he has rescued us from the dominion of darkness and brought us into the kingdom of the Son he loves, in whom we have redemption, the forgiveness of sins.

Colossians 1:13, 14 (NIV)

Forgive Others

Be kind and compassionate to one another, forgiving each other, just as in Christ God forgave you.

Ephesians 4:32 (NIV)

In Christ, You are a forgiven person.

All of your sins—past, present and future—have been forgiven once and for all.

It is Finished!
John 19:30

This is Righteousness...

Righteousness is From God.

For in the gospel the righteousness of God is revealed—a righteousness that is by faith from first to last, just as it is written: "The righteous will live by faith."

Romans 1:17 (NIV)

There is no one righteous, not even one.

Romans 3:10 (NIV)

Righteousness is a Gift

Therefore no one will be declared righteous in God's sight by the works of the law; rather, through the law we become conscious of our sin.

Romans 3:20 (NIV)

I do not set aside the grace of God, for if righteousness could be gained through the law, Christ died for nothing!

Galatians 2:21 (NIV)

But now apart from the law the righteousness of God has been made known, to which the Law and the Prophets testify. This righteousness is given through faith in Jesus Christ to all who believe. There is no difference between Jew and Gentile, for all have sinned and fall short of the glory of God, and all are justified freely by his grace through the redemption that came by Christ Jesus.

Romans 3:21-24 (NIV)

For if, by the trespass of the one man, death reigned through that one man, how much more will those who receive God's abundant provision of grace and of the gift of righteousness reign in life through the one man, Jesus Christ!

Romans 5:17 (NIV)

Christ is the culmination of the law so that there may be righteousness for everyone who believes.

Romans 10:4 (NIV)

Righteousness is Received by Faith

However, to the one who does not work but trusts God who justifies the ungodly, their faith is credited as righteousness.

Romans 4:5 (NIV)

What then shall we say? That the Gentiles, who did not pursue righteousness, have obtained it, a righteousness that is by faith; but the people of Israel, who pursued the law as the way of righteousness, have not attained their goal. Why not? Because they pursued it not by faith but as if it were by works. They stumbled over the stumbling stone.

Romans 9:30-32 (NIV)

Indeed, I count everything as loss because of the surpassing worth of knowing Christ Jesus my Lord. For his sake I have suffered the loss of all things and count them as rubbish, in order that I may gain Christ and be found in him, not having a righteousness of my own that comes from the law, but that which comes through faith in Christ, the righteousness from God that depends on faith—

Philippians 3:8, 9

You Have the Righteousness of Jesus Christ

God made him who had no sin to be sin for us, so that in him we might become the righteousness of God.

2 Corinthians 5:21 (NIV)

But thanks be to God, that you who were once slaves of sin have become obedient from the heart to the standard of teaching to which you were committed, and, having been set free from sin, have become slaves of righteousness.

Romans 6:17, 18

You are as righteous as Jesus Christ!

God justified you and declared you right in his sight because of the finished work of Jesus Christ.

This Is Life...

Man's Deepest Problem

As for you, you were dead in your transgressions and sins...

Ephesians 2:1 (NIV)

Therefore, just as sin entered the world through one man, and death through sin, and in this way death came to all men, because all sinned...

Romans 5:12 (NIV)

Death is the Problem

The wages of sin is death…

Life is the Answer

But the free gift of God is eternal life
in Christ Jesus our Lord.

"For God so loved the world,
that he gave his only Son,
that whoever believes in him
should not perish but have eternal life."
John 3:16 (NIV)

Jesus Came to Give Life

I am the gate; whoever enters through me will be saved. They will come in and go out, and find pasture., The thief comes only to steal and kill and destroy; **I have come that they may have life, and have it to the full.** I am the good shepherd. The good shepherd lays down his life for the sheep.

John 10:9-11 (NIV)

For as the Father raises the dead and gives them life, so also the Son gives life to whom he will.

John 5:21

You are Saved by the Life of Christ

For if while we were enemies we were reconciled to God by the death of his Son, much more, now that we are reconciled, shall we be saved by his life.

Romans 5:10

But because of his great love for us, God, who is rich in mercy, made us alive with Christ even when we were dead in transgressions—it is by grace you have been saved.

Ephesians 2:4, 5

I tell you the truth, whoever hears my word and believes him who sent me has eternal life and will not be condemned; he has crossed over from death to life.

John 5:24

YOU WERE DEAD IN SIN; NOW YOU ARE ALIVE IN HIM.

Whoever has the Son has life; whoever does not have the Son of God does not have life.
1 John 5:12

Jesus Christ is Your Life

When Christ who is your life appears, then you also will appear with him in glory.

Colossians 3:4 (NIV)

To them God chose to make known how great among the Gentiles are the riches of the glory of this mystery, which is Christ in you, the hope of glory.

Colossians 1:27 (NIV)

I have been crucified with Christ. It is no longer I who live, but Christ who lives in me. And the life I now live in the flesh I live by faith in the Son of God, who loved me and gave himself for me.

Galatians 2:20 (NIV)

Jesus Christ Guarantees Your Eternal Life

God has said, "Never will I leave you; never will I forsake you."

Hebrews 13:5 (NIV)

And this is the testimony, that God gave us eternal life, and this life is in his Son. Whoever has the Son has life; whoever does not have the Son of God does not have life. I write these things to you who believe in the name of the Son of God so **that you may know you have eternal life.**

1 John 5:11-13

In Christ, You are Complete

You have been given fullness in Christ, who is the head over every power and authority.

Colossians 2:10 (NIV)

His divine power has given us everything we need for life and godliness through our knowledge of him who called us by his own glory and goodness.

2 Peter 1:3 (NIV)

You Are Fully Alive in Christ

I tell you the truth, whoever hears my word and
believes him who sent me has eternal life and will not
be condemned; he has crossed over from death to life.
John 5:24 (NIV)

Then Jesus declared, "I am the bread of life.
Whoever comes to me will never go hungry,
and whoever believes in me will never be thirsty."
John 6:35 (NIV)

Jesus Christ is Fully Alive in You

To them God chose to make known how great among
the Gentiles are the riches of the glory of this mystery,
which is Christ in you, the hope of glory.
1 Colossians 1:27 (NIV)

But he who is joined to the Lord
becomes one spirit with him.
1 Corinthians 6:17

This Is Identity...

You are a New Creation

For we are his workmanship, created in Christ Jesus for good works, which God prepared beforehand, that we would walk in them.

Ephesians 2:10

Therefore, if anyone is in Christ, he is a new creation. The old has passed away; behold, the new has come.

2 Corinthians 5:17

You are a child of God

But to all who did receive him, who believed in his name, he gave the right to become children of God, who were born, not of blood nor of the will of the flesh nor of the will of man, but of God.

John 1:12, 13

See what kind of love the Father has given to us, that we should be called children of God; and so we are. The reason why the world does not know us is that it did not know him. Beloved, we are God's children now, and what we will be has not yet appeared; but we know that when he appears we shall be like him, because we shall see him as he is.

1 John 3:1, 2

WHO ARE YOU?

Do you find your worth as a parent, an executive, an athlete, or do you see yourself as a sinner, unloveable, and unworthy?

God does not identify you as any of those labels. He has named you as a child of God.

Once you accept your identity in Christ, you will never be disappointed or disillusioned about your worth.

To begin to understand who you are, consider these words of God:

His divine power has granted us all things that pertain to life and godliness, through the knowledge of him who called us to his own glory and excellence. 2 Peter 1:3

You Have Been Adopted as a Son

But when the fullness of time had come, God sent forth his Son, born of woman, born under the law, to redeem those who were under the law, so that we might receive adoption as sons.

Galatians 4:4, 5

For you did not receive the spirit of slavery to fall back into fear, but you have received the Spirit of adoption as sons, by whom we cry, "Abba! Father!"

Romans 8:15

You are a New Creation, Fully Loved by God.

Therefore, if anyone is in Christ, he is a new creation...
2 Corinthians 5:17a

You are in Christ and Christ is in You.

You are an Heir of the New Covenant

So you are no longer a slave, but a son, and if a son, then an heir through God.

Galatians 4:7

The Spirit himself bears witness with our spirit that we are children of God, and if children, then heirs—heirs of God and fellow heirs with Christ, provided we suffer with him in order that we may also be glorified with him.

Romans 8:16, 17

51

You are Saved Completely

Therefore he is able to save completely those who come to God through him, because he always lives to intercede for them.

Hebrews 7:25 NIV

You are Totally Forgiven

I am writing to you, little children, because your sins are forgiven for his name's sake.

1 John 2:12

You are Totally Cleansed

But if we walk in the light, as he is in the light, we have fellowship with one another, and the blood of Jesus his Son cleanses us from all sin.

1 John 1:7

You are Not Condemned

There is therefore no condemnation for those who are in Christ Jesus.

Romans 8:1

You are Made Perfect

For by a single offering he has perfected for all time those who are being sanctified.

Hebrews 10:14

You are at Peace with God

Therefore, since we have been justified by faith, we have peace with God through our Lord Jesus Christ.

Romans 5:1

You are a Citizen of Heaven

But our citizenship is in heaven, and from it we await a Savior, the Lord Jesus Christ...

Philippians 3:20

You are Led by the Holy Spirit

For all who are led by the Spirit of God are sons of God.

Romans 8:14

As a Child of God
You Have a New Purpose

He has made us competent as ministers of a new
covenant—not of the letter but of the Spirit;
for the letter kills, but the Spirit gives life.

2 Corinthians 3:6 (NIV)

All this is from God,
who reconciled us to himself through Christ
and gave us the ministry of reconciliation: that
God was reconciling the world to himself in Christ,
not counting men's sins against them.
And he has committed to us
the message of reconciliation.

2 Corinthians 5:18, 19 (NIV)

But you are a chosen race, a royal priesthood, a holy
nation, a people for his own possession, that you
may proclaim the excellencies of him who called you
out of darkness into his marvelous light.

1 Peter 2:9

This is the Christian Life...

This is Faith

Now faith is the assurance of things hoped for, the conviction of things not seen... And without faith it is impossible to please him, for whoever would draw near to God must believe that he exists and that he rewards those who seek him.

Hebrews 11:1, 6

So faith comes from hearing, and hearing through the word of Christ.

Romans 10:17

The righteous shall live by faith.

Galatians 3:11

...let us run with endurance the race that is set before us, looking to Jesus, the founder and perfecter of our faith, who for the joy that was set before him endured the cross, despising the shame, and is seated at the right hand of the throne of God.

Hebrews 12:1, 2

And if Christ has not been raised, your faith is futile and you are still in your sins.

1 Corinthians 15:17

THE CHRISTIAN LIFE

It is anchored in hope...

It is lived by faith in Jesus Christ...

It is expressed in love!

Faith is Resting in Christ

Come to me, all who labor and are heavy laden, and I will give you rest. Take my yoke upon you, and learn from me, for I am gentle and lowly in heart, and you will find rest for your souls. For my yoke is easy, and my burden is light."

Matthew 11:28-30

So then, there remains a Sabbath rest for the people of God, for whoever has entered God's rest has also rested from his works as God did from his.

Hebrews 4:9, 10

Faith is Being Led by the Spirit

For all who are led by the Spirit of God are sons of God.

Romans 8:14

But I say, walk by the Spirit, and you will not gratify the desires of the flesh.

Galatians 5:16

But the fruit of the Spirit is love, joy, peace, patience, kindness, goodness, faithfulness, gentleness, self-control; against such things there is no law.

Galatians 5:22, 23

Faith is Abiding in Christ

I am the vine; you are the branches. Whoever abides in me and I in him, he it is that bears much fruit, for apart from me you can do nothing.

John 15:5

Whoever confesses that Jesus is the Son of God, God abides in him, and he in God. So we have come to know and to believe the love that God has for us. God is love, and whoever abides in love abides in God, and God abides in him. By this is love perfected with us, so that we may have confidence for the day of judgment, because as he is so also are we in this world.

1 John 4:15-17

I have been crucified with Christ. It is no longer I who live, but Christ who lives in me. And the life I now live in the flesh I live by faith in the Son of God, who loved me and gave himself for me.

Galatians 2:20

This is Hope

Jesus Christ is Our Hope

To them God chose to make known how great among the Gentiles are the riches of the glory of this mystery, which is Christ in you, the hope of glory.

Colossians 1:27

When Christ who is your life appears, then you also will appear with him in glory.

Colossians 3:4

Hope is Experienced in the New Covenant

For on the one hand, a former commandment is set aside because of its weakness and uselessness for the law made nothing perfect; but on the other hand, a better hope is introduced, through which we draw near to God.

Hebrews 7:18,19

Since we have such a hope, we are very bold, not like Moses, who would put a veil over his face so that the Israelites might not gaze at the outcome of what was being brought to an end. But their minds were hardened. For to this day, when they read the old covenant, that same veil remains unlifted, because only through Christ is it taken away. Yes, to this day whenever Moses is read a veil lies over their hearts. But when one turns to the Lord, the veil is removed. Now the Lord is the Spirit, and where the Spirit of the Lord is, there is freedom. And we all, with unveiled face, beholding the glory of the Lord, are being transformed into the same image from one degree of glory to another. For this comes from the Lord who is the Spirit.

2 Corinthians 3:12-18

The Holy Spirit Guarantees Your Hope

In him you also, when you heard the word of truth, the gospel of your salvation, and believed in him, were sealed with the promised Holy Spirit, who is the guarantee of our inheritance until we acquire possession of it, to the praise of his glory.

Ephesians 1:13, 14

Hope is Your Anchor for Daily Living

Beloved, we are God's children now, and what we will be has not yet appeared; but we know that when he appears we shall be like him, because we shall see him as he is. And everyone who thus hopes in him purifies himself as he is pure.

1 John 3:2, 3

We have this as a sure and steadfast anchor of the soul, a hope that enters into the inner place behind the curtain, where Jesus has gone as a forerunner on our behalf, having become a high priest forever after the order of Melchizedek.

Hebrews 6:19, 20

We always thank God, the Father of our Lord Jesus Christ, when we pray for you, since we heard of your faith in Christ Jesus and of the love that you have for all the saints, because of the hope laid up for you in heaven.

Colossians 1:3-5

This is Love

God is Love

Beloved, let us love one another, for love is from God, and whoever loves has been born of God and knows God. Anyone who does not love does not know God, because God is love.

1 John 4:7, 8

There is no fear in love, but perfect love casts out fear. For fear has to do with punishment, and whoever fears has not been perfected in love. We love because he first loved us.

1 John 4:18, 19

God's Love Is

Love is patient and kind; love does not envy or boast; it is not arrogant or rude. It does not insist on its own way; it is not irritable or resentful; it does not rejoice at wrongdoing, but rejoices with the truth. Love bears all things, believes all things, hopes all things, endures all things. Love never ends.

1 Corinthians 13:4-8

So now faith, hope, and love abide, these three; but the greatest of these is love.

1 Corinthians 13:13

Greater love has no one than this: to lay down one's life for one's friends.

John 15:13 (NIV)

God's Love is in Your Heart

...and hope does not put us to shame, because God's love has been poured into our hearts through the Holy Spirit who has been given to us.

Romans 5:5

Nothing Can Separate You from the Love of God

For I am sure that neither death nor life, nor angels nor rulers, nor things present nor things to come, nor powers, nor height nor depth, nor anything else in all creation, will be able to separate us from the love of God in Christ Jesus our Lord.

Romans 8:38, 39

Abide in the Love of Jesus Christ

As the Father has loved me, so have I loved you. Abide in my love.

John 15:9

For this reason I bow my knees before the Father, from whom every family in heaven and on earth is named, that according to the riches of his glory he may grant you to be strengthened with power through his Spirit in your inner being, so that Christ may dwell in your hearts through faith—that you, being rooted and grounded in love, may have strength to comprehend with all the saints what is the breadth and length and height and depth, and to know the love of Christ that surpasses knowledge, that you may be filled with all the fullness of God.

Ephesians 3:14-19

Walk in Love

And walk in love, as Christ loved us and gave himself up for us, a fragrant offering and sacrifice to God.

Ephesians 5:2

For in Christ Jesus neither circumcision nor uncircumcision counts for anything, but only faith working through love.

Galatians 5:6

For you were called to freedom, brothers. Only do not use your freedom as an opportunity for the flesh, but through love serve one another.

Galatians 5:13

The World Will Know

A new commandment I give to you, that you love one another: just as I have loved you, you also are to love one another. By this all people will know that you are my disciples, if you have love for one another.

John 13:34, 35

Dive Deeper Into the Grace of God

Order Simple Gospel, Simply Grace
and the companion Study Guide

simplegospelsimplygrace.com

BASICGOSPEL

Hear it. Believe it. Live it.

The Gospel of Jesus Christ is simple, powerful, and life changing. It declares the love of God for mankind. It is the good news people long to hear. Radio delivers it straight to the heart.

But it is not enough just to hear the good news. God wants to make His love a reality in our lives. He wants us to believe it and live it.

At Basic Gospel, we are dedicated to proclaiming the name of Jesus Christ and the profound simplicity of His love and grace.

Our hope is that the clear presentation of the basic Gospel and the singular focus on the death, burial and resurrection of Jesus Christ will anchor listeners to the love of God and will encourage them to experience the fullness of the New Covenant life that is theirs in Christ.

Bob Christopher, Bob Davis, and Richard Peifer, occasionally joined by Andrew Farley, can be heard daily at 3pm U.S. Central time on hundreds of radio stations across the United States and Canada. To find a station near you please see our current station log online at basicgospel.net/stations. You can also listen to the live stream or archive on our website.

You can join the conversation while we're on the air by calling, 844.322.2742 between 3:00 and 3:30 pm U.S. Central time. If you can't call in live, please leave a voice mail at the same number (844.322.2742) or send an email to bob@basicgospel.net

Like us on Facebook – fb.com/basicgospel
and follow us on Twitter @basicgospelrdo

87729426R00037

Made in the USA
Columbia, SC
18 January 2018